D0402131

The World According to

MICHAEL MOORE

AN UNAUTHORIZED PORTRAIT
IN HIS OWN WORDS

KEN LAWRENCE

Andrews McMeel
Publishing

Kansas City

04 05 06 07 08 BBB 10 9 8 7 6 5 4 3 2 1

ISBN: 0-7407-5122-0

Library of Congress Control Number: 2004111074

Book design and composition by Kelly & Company, Lee's Summit, Missouri

ATTENTION: SCHOOLS AND BUSINESSES

Andrews McMeel books are available at quantity discounts with bulk purchase for educational, business, or sales promotional use. For information, please write to: Special Sales Department, Andrews McMeel Publishing, 4520 Main Street, Kansas City, Missouri 64111.

CONTENTS

INTRODUCTION

One of the most recognizable figures in popular culture today, Michael Moore never fails to inspire fervent debate. With the success of his latest provocative documentary, *Fahrenheit 9/11,* Moore has once again entertained, enlightened, and infuriated audiences with his trademark brand of humor, satire, and cutting-edge political commentary.

Born in 1954 in Davison, Michigan, a suburb of Flint—at the time home to one of General Motors' largest car factories—Moore grew up in a working-class Irish-Catholic family. His father and grandfather both worked at the GM plant, and Moore attended parochial school until he was 14, when he transferred to Davison High School. To earn a Boy Scout merit badge, Moore once created a slide show explaining how businesses polluted the environment. Some say this was the start of his political activism.

As an 18-year-old high school senior in 1972, Moore ran for and won a seat on the Flint School Board and became one of the youngest people in the country to hold public office. After graduating, Moore was expected to go to work in the GM factory, like his father and grandfather before him. When the day arrived, however, he panicked and decided that factory work was not for him. He briefly attended the University of Michigan at Flint but then dropped out to focus on his political activities.

In 1976, Moore started working at the alternative newspaper the *Flint Voice*. Later, under his editorship, it became the *Michigan Voice* and grew into one of the country's most respected and admired alternative newspapers. About 10 years later, Moore was offered a position at the large national counterculture magazine *Mother Jones* in San Francisco, but his stint there was short-lived. After penning an article about an autoworker, he began to disagree with management about the magazine's direction. Reportedly, he refused to publish an article critical of the Nicaraguan Sandinistas, a story he believed was inaccurate and unfair, and he was fired. He had been there less than two years.

Sinking into a depression, Moore watched movies almost nonstop to keep his mind off his problems. It was during this time that he got the idea to return to Flint armed with a camera. He thought perhaps he could get his ideas across better on film than with the written word.

As Moore tells it, he was watching TV when he heard about GM closing the Flint plant, despite the company's huge profits. Feeling this was unfair to workers and the rest of the city, he decided to make a film about how the plant's closing affected Flint. He was naive enough to think that he could ride around with GM's chairman, Roger Smith, and discuss with him, on camera, the ripple effect of the plant's demise.

Moore sold his house and used some of his settlement money from *Mother Jones* to finance the film, but repeated attempts to interview Smith fell through. Undeterred, Michael turned his clips about trying to interview Smith into *Roger & Me*, a tongue-in-cheek documentary about corporate greed. The 1989 low-budget movie made history, becoming one of the largest grossing documentaries at the time and breaking ground in the genre. Until then, most documentaries were dry and somber. Although *Roger & Me* dealt with a serious topic, it was very funny.

After the financial and critical success of *Roger & Me*, Moore worked on several small films and eventually made a full feature film with John Candy titled *Canadian Bacon*. The satire's story line hinged on the United States declaring a "Cold War" against Canada. Because of Candy's death shortly after the film was finished, it was mired in litigation and never enjoyed wide release.

In 1994, Moore turned to television with *TV Nation* on NBC. Although the show was critically acclaimed, its ratings and biting commentaries were not to the network's taste, and NBC dropped it after one season. FOX picked it up, but once again, the show suffered from low ratings and was canceled again after one season.

Reacting to the nation's corporate downsizing trend, in 1996 Moore wrote *Downsize This! Random Threats from an Unarmed American,* which hit the best-seller lists nationwide. In 1997, while on his book tour, Moore tried his hand at documentaries again by making *The Big One,* a look at economic unfairness in the country, but it did not rise to the level of *Roger & Me.*

Moore returned to television in 1999 with *The Awful Truth,* a satiric look at current events, similar to his *TV Nation.* Unable to find funding for the satire about the United States within the country itself, Moore eventually received backing from the British network Channel Four, and the show ran on the cable channel Bravo for two seasons.

Exasperated by the 2000 election debacle and the administration of George W. Bush, Moore returned to print with *Stupid White Men . . . and Other Sorry Excuses for the State of the Nation!,* which was scheduled for publication in fall 2001. When the 9/11 terrorist attacks occurred, publisher HarperCollins ordered Moore to tone down the book's criticism of President Bush, but he refused. The company then threatened to scrap the book if Moore didn't censor himself and get in line with what it perceived as the nation's mood. For a while it looked like the book would never be published, but Moore got lucky.

While giving a presentation before a group of librarians he mentioned his "upcoming" book. After he explained the situation, one librarian began an e-mail campaign that was picked up by her colleagues. The librarians saw the issue as one of censorship, and they backed Moore. The group put pressure on HarperCollins to publish the book just as Moore had written it. Bowing to the pressure of the powerful book-buying bloc, HarperCollins released *Stupid White Men* in spring 2002. It became an instant best-seller.

That fall, Moore released *Bowling for Columbine,* a critical look at guns and America's culture of violence. It became the first documentary to be shown at the Cannes Film Festival in almost 50 years and won the festival's Jury Prize. The movie also won the 2002 Oscar for Best Documentary, and Moore lambasted President Bush and the war in Iraq during his acceptance speech. The incident drew strong reaction from both sides of the issue and put Moore at the center of a political firestorm.

But Moore's crowning film achievement was yet to come.

With the nation divided on support for the war in Iraq and President Bush's performance on the economy and the fight against terrorism, *Fahrenheit 9/11,* a scathing investigation of the war and Bush's questionable relationship with the Saudi royal family and the bin Laden family, was set for release in spring 2004.

The movie received a 20-minute standing ovation and won the Palm d'Or at the 2004 Cannes Film Festival, the first documentary to win this top prize. But Moore faced trouble at home when the Walt Disney Co. prohibited its subsidiary Miramax from distributing the film. After lengthy negotiations, Miramax heads Bob and Harvey Weinstein bought out Disney's contract and the movie was distributed in June 2004 by the Weinsteins' company, Fellowship Adventure Group, IFC Films and Lion's Gate.

Fahrenheit 9/11 opened to sold-out theaters and made over $20 million in ticket sales during its first weekend, not only eclipsing the financial success of *Bowling for Columbine* but also becoming the largest grossing documentary of all time.

Michael Moore is steadfast in his beliefs and is clearly passionate about his work. Although Moore may seem radical to some, the American public pays attention to what he has to say.

Here, then, is Michael Moore in his own words.

ON PRESIDENT GEORGE W. BUSH

I can't believe we've got a guy sitting in the White House who did not win the White House. And I will never get over that. I will never be silent about it.

—*Los Angeles Times,* March 7, 2002

He's a serial liar. . . . He lied to the country about weapons of mass destruction, about chemical and biological weapons in Iraq, about Saddam Hussein having something to do with September 11, and on and on and on and on and on.

—*Lou Dobbs Tonight,* October 14, 2003

I think the Bushes are beholden to the Saudi royals. I think it's one of the reasons why Prince Bandar, the Saudi ambassador, could call up the White House within 24 hours of September 11th and say, "I would like a free ride out of the country for 24 members of the bin Laden family and 140 Saudi royals," and the White House said, "Sure."

—*The Daily Show,* June 6, 2004

You know, they have such a close relationship that the Saudi royal family refers to his dad as Bandar Bush. They've actually given him his own nickname within the royal family. This is how close they are.

—*Democracy Now!,* October 15, 2003

Nobody approves of this guy; he wasn't even elected by the people. This was a coup of immeasurable proportions. We should be so outraged and continue our outrage no matter who you voted for.

—Speech before the Commonwealth Club, March 4, 2002

I don't have to worry about the entertainment. Bush provided all the entertainment in the movie. The funniest lines in [*Fahrenheit 9/11*] are his. I give him his props for that. . . . You know, I couldn't write lines like the ones that he speaks.

—*The Tavis Smiley Show,* June 29, 2004

The first day of baseball season Enron Field opened down in Houston, right? So Bush takes the Enron jet back there. And I'm reading this story and I'm thinking, "Oh, probably to throw out the first pitch." Right? No, Kenny Boy [Kenneth Lay, former chairman of Enron] was throwing out the first pitch. [Bush] just wanted to be there to watch.

—*The Daily Show,* February 21, 2002

That's a home-video VHS that the teacher set on a tripod. And I'm telling you, we're being kind to Bush. You should see the longer version [in *Fahrenheit 9/11*] where I let it run for, like, three of the seven minutes. It is painful. Painful!

—*Entertainment Weekly,* July 9, 2004

Moore went to the White House to drop off a copy of his book *Dude, Where's My Country?* After being told through a speaker box to mail his book to the president, Moore asked the driver of a mini-van that was going through the gate to deliver it.

"Can you give a copy of my book to the president? No word has more than three syllables!" He was turned down.

"I thought they'd at least take it from me if only just to inspect for typos. Typos can be a threat to homeland security."

—*Washington Post,* October 11, 2003

ON THE 9/11 ATTACK

If you just think about this, and this is all coming from a cave in Afghanistan? I mean, I can't get a cell phone from here to Queens, so exactly how did the mastermind of all evil put this together? I'm not saying he didn't have something to do with it or wasn't involved or whatever, I just think it's a legitimate question to ask.

—*Democracy Now!,* October 15, 2003

I want justice done to anybody involved in this. And to those who weren't doing their job to try and prevent this, I want them removed.

—*The Daily Show,* February 21, 2002

When it's that perfect, and 15 of 19 are from one country, a country with very close relations and financial dealings, what the hell is going on? I'm not saying even if they are involved, "Let's go bomb Saudi Arabia." But let's call this for what it is.

—*Denver Post,* October 18, 2002

They're murderers and should be brought to justice. But let's get a handle on this, folks. You've got the Bush administration using that event in such a disrespectful and immoral way. They're using the deaths of those people to try and shred our civil liberties, change our Constitution, round people up. That's not how you honor them, by using them to change our way of life as a free country.

—*60 Minutes,* June 27, 2004

Why don't we call this multi-millionaire terrorism? Why don't we look at bin Laden as a multi-millionaire first, instead of someone who practices Islam? That's what he is; he's a multi-millionaire. Those weren't poor peasants flying those planes. This was a military operation, funded by people in a government that's been friendly to the Bush family for 40 years.

—*South Florida Sun-Sentinel,*
October 20, 2002

Let me ask you this, "Do you believe any of those things strongly enough to fly a plane at 500 miles an hour into a building?" No, you don't. Neither do I. But your enemy does. And if your enemy does, who eventually wins? That's a chilling question that we don't want to face.

—*Rocky Mountain News,* October 19, 2002

If anything, Sept. 11 just confirmed what I was already saying in [*Bowling for Columbine*]: That we have this culture of violence that we're both master and victim of. And because we're the master, we can actually alter the victim part. We can choose to be different. We can choose to treat the rest of the world differently. We can actually make it better. A lot of countries can't say that. We can say it. Why don't we do it?

—*Toronto Star,* September 7, 2002

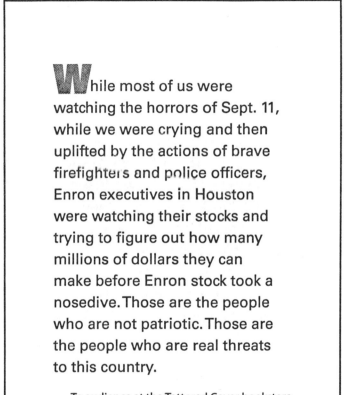

While most of us were watching the horrors of Sept. 11, while we were crying and then uplifted by the actions of brave firefighters and police officers, Enron executives in Houston were watching their stocks and trying to figure out how many millions of dollars they can make before Enron stock took a nosedive. Those are the people who are not patriotic. Those are the people who are real threats to this country.

—To audience at the Tattered Cover bookstore in Denver on March 9, 2002, as reported by the *Denver Post*, March 10, 2002

The rich are always wanting to get rid of us. The rich did 9/11—it wasn't the poor of the world who killed 3,000 Americans . . . and they were led by a millionaire, Osama bin Laden, and financed in part by the Saudi royal family. . . . We focus on [bin Laden's] Arabness, his religious affiliation, but not on his money.

—*Sacramento Bee,* October 23, 2003

ON LIBERALS AND CONSERVATIVES

The conservatives and tho right-wingers, the one thing you've got to admire about them is they actually believe in something and they never stop believing in it. They wake up in the morning and they greet the dawn believing in it. We don't ever even see the dawn.

—Speech before the Commonwealth Club,
March 4, 2002

The only socialists, or whatever that word means, the only people, in other words, I guess, who you believe want governments to take care of them are the Bushes and the Cheneys and the WorldComs and the Enrons. They are the people who want the government to give them the tax breaks, to make sure they don't have to pay their taxes, to let them move their corporate headquarters to Bermuda or the Cayman Islands.

—*Crossfire,* August 8, 2002

Unlike most of the left, I have reached a wide mainstream audience, something the left doesn't usually reach. And that is dangerous, and they need to stop that.

—*Fort McMurray Today* (Edmonton, Alberta), June 22, 2004

I think it's time that the liberal leaders are just thanked for their efforts and asked to go away.

—*Minneapolis Star Tribune,* October 8, 1996

We're too lazy to get out of bed. This is our problem. Conservatives are up at, like, six in the morning. They're up to greet the sunrise and screw the poor. They're kicking ass and taking names by the time we're still looking for a cappuccino.

—*Times* (London), October 25, 2002

So, you know, I'm very optimistic about our fellow Americans. The problem is they just don't have anybody to vote for. They're liberal on the issues, but where are the liberal leaders?

—*Democracy Now!*, October 15, 2003

So many people who call themselves liberals are willing to compromise and just give in and just start doing the backward shuffle.

—Speech before the Commonwealth Club,
March 4, 2002

You have to understand when you come from Flint, Michigan, there is no left. There is no left community, no cafe to go to and order a latte and talk about this stuff. The politics I have come from growing up in an Irish-Catholic working-class factory family.

—*Los Angeles Times,* March 7, 2002

Liberals who say, "I'm going to send her to the inner-city school to make things better," are so misguided politically. Your little five-year-old did not create the racist, segregated, class-based society we live in.

—*Playboy,* July 1, 1999

I moved here [to New York City] in the early '90s, and the city is today in many respects a much better place to live. Liberals don't like to admit that, but it's true.

—*New York Daily News,* April 11, 1999

ON AMERICA

Anytime there's a new invention all the entrepreneurs just go for it and, because of this great economic system we have called capitalism, the mediocre rise to the top, so you end up with VHS instead of Beta, you end up with IBMs instead of Apple. The most mediocre wins. It's kind of the Darwinism of this kind of economic system.

—Responses to questions from the
audience after a speech at the
Commonwealth Club, March 4, 2002

We've got two million people in prison now. You know, that's the easy way to go. . . . The hard way to go is to say, "You know what? If we work toward full employment and if we had a safety net to catch anybody who wasn't employed, where we made sure everybody had the means to get through the day and the week and the month, we would have an enormous decrease in crime."

—To audience in the Showcase Cinema West movie theater in Flint, Michigan, at the home-town premiere of *Bowling for Columbine*, cited by AlterNet.org, November 20, 2002

Most of us know that for a country that has such incredible ideals, we have not lived up to them in many ways. The patriotic thing to do is to aspire to [make] this country the one that our founding fathers thought it should be. Anybody who works hard to do that, whether they're conservative or liberal, is doing the work of a true American.

—*Entertainment Weekly,* July 9, 2004

There's millions of you on the sidelines, and I'm like the coach saying, "Come on, bench, get in the game!"

—*Time,* July 12, 2004

I'm a citizen in a democracy. To call me an activist would be redundant. It's not a spectator sport. If we all become non-participants, it no longer works.

—*Interview,* November 1, 2002

Collectively, as a society, we endorse being sold fear. Corporations, the media . . . so many different groups benefit from the public being afraid.

—*Boston Globe,* October 27, 2002

Look, I really think that we should aspire to be more Canadian. If we did, we'd be living in a safer, saner country. And you gotta admire any group of people who'd put a leaf on their flag.

—*Entertainment Weekly,* October 25, 2002

Their attitude is, "We're all Canadians. We each have a responsibility to each other. Why? Because we're Canadians, dammit!" Our ethic? "Every man for himself. Pull yourself up by your bootstraps." It creates this stress. . . . We've got a quarter-billion guns in our homes. So somebody gets depressed, something happens with a neighbor, somebody doesn't like what happens at work, and there's the gun. Seventy percent of our murders are between people who know each other.

—*Philadelphia Inquirer,* October 22, 2002

If the people could be made to believe that the enemy was everywhere and could strike at any moment, they would give the leader whatever he wanted. Freedom. Civil liberties. I believe that's the approach that these guys—Bush, Ashcroft, Cheney, and their cronies—are taking, using Sept. 11 as a means to push through their agenda, to get everybody frightened so that they'll just let them do whatever they want to do.

—*South Florida Sun-Sentinel,*
October 20, 2002

We've taken our liberties for granted so long and our freedom to have it our way. We can all buy our flags and our little bumper stickers and we've got this "rah, rah, America" thing going on. But if it really came to it, are you going to stand up for what this country's about, your freedom and democracy?

—*Rocky Mountain News,* October 19, 2002

If everyone had a decent job and was making $50,000 a year then they would own their own home, have transportation, and be able to send their children to school. Then what are the chances of the guy living next door to you breaking into your home and stealing your TV? None. What's the chance of someone making $50,000 a year sticking you up on the street? None. Why wouldn't you support people being paid a decent wage just for your own safety?

—*Chicago Sun-Times,* October 3, 2002

The mass majority of Americans say they want stronger environmental laws, they believe in women's rights, they want gun control laws; go down the whole list, they are very liberal on the issues.

—*The Daily Show,* June 6, 2004

The problem is not Roger Smith, nor General Motors, it's an economic system that's not just or fair, and we can't have democracy until it is.

—*Independent* (London), February 25, 1990

I'm always optimistic at the beginning of a year. It starts wearing off around the State of the Union Address.

—*Chicago Tribune,* December 25, 1994

The best thing about the Midwest is the total lack of pretension. You don't get that in New York or Los Angeles. People are exactly who they are.

—*Chicago Tribune,* August 30, 1994

I don't think you can separate violence, whether it's the husband who beats his wife or a corporation that builds a missile that's going to kill thousands of people. There's something about us where we've tacitly condoned violence as a means to an end.

—*Rocky Mountain News,* March 7, 2002

The American Dream is gone. People are working harder for longer hours, less money, and no sense of security. That's the way it's been the last 10 or 15 years.

—*Cleveland Plain Dealer,* July 25, 1994

I think that the American public is a lot smarter than Hollywood believes that it is. You only need to go as far as the Top 10 shows from last week to see what they're watching. They don't watch the dumb shows. They watch *Rose-anne,* they watch *Seinfeld,* they watch *Grace Under Fire,* and they watch *60 Minutes.*

—*Dallas Morning News,* July 19, 1994

There's something about working-class satire and irony that seems to be missing from our national language.

—*American Demographics,* January 1998

People have had it with keeping silent for the past six months. They resent having felt like if they chose to question what the government is up to or, God forbid, dissent, they would somehow be considered unpatriotic.

—An e-mail from Michael Moore to supporters
as cited by the *Guardian,* March 27, 2002

We live in a country that is ironically illiterate.

—*South Florida Sun-Sentinel,*
April 10, 1999

ON *THE AWFUL TRUTH*

I see the show as [a cross between] the World Wrestling Federation and C-SPAN. If you can kind of imagine those two together, that's what we're doing.

—CNN.com, April 27, 1999

In one episode, Moore convinces a company to rehire a man they had fired for being in a demonstration.

"Occasionally, we'll have those successes. But it is okay if it's just hilarious."

—*Toronto Sun,* May 15, 1999

I'm all for the retro-commie thing—I've subtitled *The Awful Truth,* The People's Democratic Republic of Television.

—*Scotsman,* March 3, 1999

I love the irony of it. I had to go out of America to get money for a show about America.

—*Chicago Sun-Times,* February 4, 1999

One of the main functions of satire [like in *The Awful Truth*] is to confront the uncomfortable issues. Satire is not supposed to be the kind of Comedy Lite you can find on every other channel. Satire assumes the audience has a brain.

—*Fort Worth Star-Telegram,* June 9, 1999

ON OSAMA BIN LADEN

So for all their talk about wanting to get bin Laden, they made a half-hearted attempt to do it, because they didn't want to divert resources from what their main goal was, which was to go in and invade Iraq. And that's what they've been about since Day 1.

—*CNN Live Today,* June 25, 2004

The bin Laden family and their associates over the last 30 years have invested a billion and a half dollars in the Bush family and their businesses and their associates and this is all part of the public record. You can go and look them up.

—*The Daily Show,* June 6, 2004

Six billion people on the planet [and] the guy supposedly responsible for the worst terrorist act on our soil—also his family—just happens to know quite well and have business relations with the first family of this country.

—*Democracy Now!*, October 15, 2003

ON *BOWLING FOR COLUMBINE*

On behalf of our producers, cast, Lynn Glynn and Michael Donovan from Canada, I'd like to thank the Academy for this.

I've invited my fellow documentary nominees on the stage with us. And we would like to— they are here, they are here in solidarity with me, because we like nonfiction. We like nonfiction, and we live in fictitious times. We live in the time where we have fictitious election results that elect a fictitious president. We live in a time where we have a man sending us to war for fictitious reasons, whether it's the fictions of duct tape or the fictions of Orange Alerts.

We are against this war, Mr. Bush. Shame on you, Mr. Bush. Shame on you. And any time you've got the pope and the Dixie Chicks against you, your time is up. Thank you very much.

—Acceptance speech at the 2002
Academy Awards for Best Documentary

For the next couple of months I could not walk down the street without some form of serious abuse. Threats of physical violence, people wanting to fight me, right in my face, "F———YOU! You're a traitor!" People pulling over in their cars screaming. People spitting on the sidewalk. I finally stopped going out.

—*Entertainment Weekly,* July 9, 2004

Animation gives you the freedom to say the things that need to be said. This particular section of my film, "The Brief History of the United States," has the potential to be a very bitter pill for many viewers to swallow in terms of my take on how we got to where we're at, and animation is the big spoonful of sugar that helps the medicine go down.

—*Los Angeles Times,* November 1, 2002

In Switzerland, it's the law. You have to have a gun in every house because they don't have a standing army. And last year, they had 75 murders. Clearly, it's not the proliferation of guns that is solely the cause of why we have so much murder and violence in the United States. It's something else. And it's that something else that I wanted to address in the film.

—*Milwaukee Journal Sentinel,*
October 30, 2002

The American Ethic is "fuck everybody," every man for himself . . . me, me, me, me.

And now Britain is going down the American road. You're adopting the American Ethic. I want this film to be a warning. Here's the end result of the American Ethic.

—*Time Out,* October 30, 2002

You could release this film in any given week in America and it would be timely.

—*Independent* (London), October 28, 2002

I see bowling as a very American thing, an All-American sport. The other All-American sport is violence. They went to their favorite class, bowling, in the morning. I think they just went from one to the other.

—*Boston Globe,* October 27, 2002

This is a film about America— master and victim of violence. And what we need to do to change this, because it rips apart our families and neighborhoods, and the world at large.

—*Houston Chronicle,* October 26, 2002

Schwarzenegger can kill 3,000 in a movie, and he gets a PG-13!

—*Detroit News,* October 25, 2002

I love my country. I love the people in this country, and I love being an American. I'm trying to do this to make us better.

—*South Florida Sun-Sentinel,*
October 20, 2002

I have long admired the old filmmakers who used comedy and satire as a means to discuss or illuminate social conditions, whether it was Charlie Chaplin, Will Rogers, or even the Marx Brothers. I hope people will laugh at this movie harder than they've laughed at a movie in years—but that they will also find themselves choking back the tears.

—*USA Today,* October 11, 2002

Most of what's in the film came off totally unplanned. But that's generally how I always work. I know what it is I want to say, but I don't plan out how I'm going to do it. I didn't go to film school. I only had one year of college, period. So I never learned how to write a thesis or lay things out structurally. Which makes the movie a lot more interesting. You don't know where it's going. And I don't know always where it's going, either.

—*Newsday,* October 10, 2002

Sadly, many documentaries, especially from the Left, don't have a sense of humor. I didn't want to make a lecture; I wanted to take people on an emotional roller coaster, like any good movie, with enough comedic relief to make the heavy stuff bearable. Or else I'd be as guilty as the fear-mongering media I was condemning.

—*New York Daily News,* October 6, 2002

The most shocking thing was when [Charlton] Heston looked into the camera and blurted out, "Our problem in this country is mixed ethnicity." I'm sitting there thinking, "Oh my God! I can't believe he's saying this stuff. This is my entire film."

—*Chicago Sun-Times,* October 3, 2002

I'm sure a lot of people will hate it here, but hopefully it is the right people who hate it.

—*Denver Post,* March 10, 2002

I don't want people to leave the theater depressed and in despair. Because if you're in despair, then you're paralyzed. That's why the humor's in the film. I want you to go out and do something.

—*Pittsburgh Post-Gazette,*
September 10, 2002

In my movie, I'm trying to connect the dots between the local violence and the global violence, and I think they're part and parcel of the same American way: Kill first, ask questions later.

—*Sacramento Bee,* October 25, 2002

Guns and Columbine are just my entry point into the much larger discussion that I wish would take place. I'm much more concerned about the fact that we've just gone nuts as opposed to whether we've got too many gun nuts in America.

—*Gazette,* September 9, 2002

ON PRESIDENT
BILL CLINTON

Clinton did a lot of good things, and ho did a lot of things I didn't like.

—Lou Dobbs Tonight,
October 14, 2003

When Clinton was president, I went after him. And if Kerry's president, on Day Two I'll be on him.

—Time, July 12, 2004

When he's his honest, Big-Mac-eating, sax-playing, hillbilly self, we like the guy. But some little voice in his head keeps whispering, "Moderate, Bill, moderate and people will love you." . . . What a shame. What a waste. What a wuss.

—*Columbus Dispatch,* September 15, 1996

What single fact did this multiyear, $50 million [Starr] investigation undercover? That middle-aged men have affairs with younger women. . . . I could have told you that for $50.

—*Orlando Sentinel,* April 11, 1999

ON CORPORATE GREED

If you close a factory at a time
when you made record profits,
I think that should be a crime.
I think It's immoral and obscene,
and there should be legislation
against it.

—*Ottawa Citizen,* September 27, 1996

In a more just world Phil Knight,
who runs Nike, would be made to
work in one of those Indonesian
sweatshops.

—*Minneapolis Star Tribune,* October 8, 1996

It is truly one of the beauties of capitalism that they'll sell you the rope to hang themselves, if they believe that they can make money.

—*USA Today,* July 19, 1994

It used to be if you worked hard and the company prospered, you prospered. Now, the company prospers—but you lose your job.

—CNNfn's *Before Hours,* September 17, 1996

I've never said it's wrong for people to make money nor is it wrong to be wealthy. My point is, it's wrong to be greedy, that there is such a thing as enough. If you're making a good salary or your company is making a good profit, why the hell do you have to make 1,000 families miserable and throw them out of work just so you can make a little more money than last year? . . . That's the part I don't get.

—*Dallas Morning News,* April 11, 1999

I don't think a corporation should be able to move to Mexico. I have an ethic that's more important than lower labor costs, and that's preservation of the family and people's lives. I've seen families destroyed because they've lost their jobs simply because [companies] could make a bigger buck elsewhere.

—*Orange County Register,* January 2, 1990

They're greedy! You will never hear them utter the words "enough is enough." [General Motors will] close down all the factories in this country if they believe that they're going to make more money in Mexico and Taiwan.

—*Newsday,* January 25, 1990

Air conditioning allowed the South to become a powerful and vital force. Now, they can sit in air-conditioned offices in Dallas and [mess] the world up.

—*Dallas Morning News,* September 8, 2002

ON *FAHRENHEIT 9/11*

We found that if you entered the theater on the fence, you fell off it somewhere during those two hours. It ignites a fire in people who had given up.

—*New York Times,* June 20, 2004

My point is first of all that the Bushes were so close to the Saudis that they essentially had turned a blind eye to what was really going on before 9/11. And after 9/11 they were in denial.

—*International Herald Tribune,* May 18, 2004

Last week they had a huge organized effort to harass theater owners so they wouldn't show my movie. This week it's the appeal to the FEC [Federal Election Commission] to take my ads off the air. Every time they do this they just bring more people, make them aware of the movie. So, if there is any right-wing groups listening tonight, please keep doing this.

—*The Daily Show,* June 6, 2004

We've had this [abuse of prisoners by U.S. troops] footage in our possession for two months. I saw it before any of the Abu Ghraib news broke. I think it's pretty embarrassing that a guy like me with a high school education and with no training in journalism can do this. What the hell is going on here? It's pathetic.

—*New York Times,* May 23, 2004

It is sadly very possible that many 15- and 16-year-olds will be asked and recruited to serve in Iraq in the next couple of years. If they are old enough to be recruited and capable of being in combat and risking their lives, they certainly deserve the right to see what is going on in Iraq.

—On the movie's R rating, as reported in the *Leader-Post,* June 15, 2004

Well, it's an op-ed piece. It's my opinion about the last four years of the Bush administration. And that's what I call it. I'm not trying to pretend that this is some sort of, you know, fair and balanced work of journalism, even though those who use the words "fair and balanced" often aren't that.

—ABC's *This Week*, June 20, 2004

But I hope it doesn't happen where an American filmmaker makes a film about America and it can't be seen in America. What is the message to the rest of the world then? It's not a good message, so I'm hopeful we'll shortly have an American distributor.

—CNN.com, May 6, 2004

It's a work of journalism. It's the real journalism that the journalists should be doing.

—*Fort McMurray Today* (Edmonton, Alberta), June 22, 2004

You know, I guess the way I felt after seeing all the numbers and all the exit polls and all this from the surveys they do of people coming to see it, it was clear to me that there are a lot of people in this country that want some questions answered and who are unhappy with what's going on.

—*The Tavis Smiley Show,* June 29, 2004

I encourage all teenagers to come see my movie, by any means necessary. If you need me to sneak you in, let me know.

—Associated Press, June 23, 2004

ON GUNS

I'm just asking that we, as Americans, take a look at this violent culture that wo've created. The violence that happens personally, in our communities, and globally.

—CNN.com, October 16, 2002

Every poll shows that people believe in gun control.

—*Los Angeles Times,* October 9, 2002

Out of the 11,000 gun murders in the United States I think 500 are murders because a stranger broke into the house. There are 270 million people in the country, and 500 times a stranger broke into the house and killed somebody. But here's the really interesting statistic. Out of those 500, the 200 who died were killed by their own gun because the criminal took their gun or the homeowner misfired and killed a family member. You have three times greater chance of being struck by lightning than of a stranger breaking into your house and killing you with a gun. But you're not afraid to walk in the rain, are you?

—*Milwaukee Journal Sentinel,* October 30, 2002

We could get rid of all our guns and enact a bunch of strong gun-control laws, and we would still have that shared American psyche. We would still have that common fear that the "other" is going to harm us. As long as we feel this way, we'll continue to resolve our disputes in a violent way, think of violence first instead of peaceful negotiation or compromise.

—*Houston Chronicle,* October 26, 2002

The NRA has 4 million members. I know for a fact that there are 5 million Americans who agree with me on this issue, so can I get 5 million Americans to join the basic membership and run for president against Charlton Heston and then dismantle the organization? After a couple of months I thought it would be too much work, but I had already gone ahead and bought a $750 lifetime membership.

—*Entertainment Weekly,* October 25, 2002

I've never believed in "the good German theory," that "I only drove the train to the camp." [Or in people saying] "I didn't put her on welfare." "I didn't put the gun in the uncle's house. I'm not responsible." That's the American way: "I'm not responsible. We're just selling bullets here at Kmart. We didn't kill the kids at Columbine." I want to change that.

—*Sacramento Bee,* October 25, 2002

Many guns are purchased by white people who live in the suburbs, a place that is usually safe and has low crime. Maybe it's time for white people to take a look at how we're fed these racially based fears that make us purchase guns.

—*Chicago Sun-Times,* October 3, 2002

Until we correct problems with our social conditions, it's not a good idea to have a lot of guns laying around. I support control and restriction of firearms until we can address a few of these social concerns. When we do that, we can have our guns back.

—*Rocky Mountain News,* March 7, 2002

ON THE WAR IN IRAQ

And the saddest of this all is that we have sent our kids in the military over there in this war, for what? No WMD, no connection between Saddam and 9/11; it's because they have the second largest supply of oil in the world, and how many more of them have to die for that?

—*The Daily Show,* June 6, 2004

Because I'm an American and because I pay taxes therefore I fund the invasion of Iraq. So I'm partly responsible for that. So I have to do something about it.

—*Toronto Sun,* June 20, 2004

Saying that Saddam had something to do with 9/11, this was genius, because the American people bought it. They actually believed it. It worked.

—*Democracy Now!,* October 15, 2003

The guy who's sitting in the Oval Office tonight wants to bomb. We don't need any more inspections, let's just bomb them and we'll find out later if they have the weapons. That's the American way. I don't like that. I'm an American. I paid for those bombs. And I want it stopped.

—To audience in the Showcase Cinema West movie theater in Flint, Michigan, at the home-town premiere of *Bowling for Columbine*, cited by AlterNet.org, November 20, 2002

We killed a lot of civilians, and I think that we're going to have to answer for that—whether it's now or in the hereafter. . . . They were human beings who were just trying to get on with their daily lives.

—*Entertainment Weekly,* July 9, 2004

ON THE MEDIA

Bona-fide journalists in the U.S. supported this war, cheerleaded this war, got in bed with the administration, never asked the hard questions, and completely failed the American people by not doing their job.

—*Fort McMurray Today* (Edmonton, Alberta), June 22, 2004

I'm a subversive only by default because the rest of the media haven't done their jobs.

—*Toronto Star,* April 19, 1997

Forty people a day in this country are shot and killed with guns. What about the 40 who died yesterday, or the 40 who will die tomorrow? Are they any less newsworthy, any less relevant, any less tragic? Or has the [Washington, D.C., area] sniper just made it convenient for news media to park the satellite dish in a parking lot where it's easier to do the story?

—*Philadelphia Inquirer,*
October 22, 2002

No matter what the events of the day, on the 6 o'clock news they will carry four or five stories about the sniper shootings. They call it a "package." It may run as long as 10 or 15 minutes. And I can guarantee you that at the end, you will know nothing. You will not be enlightened. What these people are doing is appealing to our basest instincts. I call it "sniper porn."

—*Detroit News,* October 19, 2002

Well, [the TV network] FOX wouldn't let me do a TV show this season, not in an election year. They were a little too concerned about what I might do to muck things up.

—*Toronto Star,* September 29, 1996

The thing about "objective" journalism is a myth. You watch the nightly news every night [and] it's one-sided. . . . On Christmas Eve . . . you don't see families evicted from their homes as you see in [*Roger & Me*].

—*Christian Science Monitor,* January 16, 1990

If the media had done their job, if they'd asked the hard questions of the Bush administration about these weapons of mass destruction, demanded proof—the media—and everybody watching this knows this—got on board. They took the soup, they took the Kool-Aid. They just became cheerleaders for this war. And that was a disservice to the American people.

—ABC's *This Week,* June 20, 2004

Roger & Me] is doing the job the *Flint Journal* should have been doing, and it's embarrassing to them.

—*Seattle Times,* January 10, 1990

There's a myth of objectivity out there, whether it's a documentary or the *Philadelphia Inquirer.* We're subjective beings by nature. Even the decision of what to put in the paper, where to place it—it's all subjective.

—*Philadelphia Inquirer,* October 22, 2002

ON HIMSELF

I didn't have any of this so-called success until I was 35 years old with *Roger & Me.* Up until that point, I never made more than $15,000 a year. When you spend the first 17 years—in other words, half—of your adult life earning $15,000 or less, it really doesn't matter what kind of success you have after that. It's so ingrained in you.

—*Time,* July 12, 2004

I'm a filmmaker trying to make a good film that's entertaining. That's ultimately what I'm doing. I am putting out my point of view. You can take it or leave it, or take some of it and leave some of it. But am I selective in what I present? Absolutely.

—*Milwaukee Journal Sentinel,* October 30, 2002

I cringe when I see myself in the movies. I have a sign on the door for the editors to read when they walk in: "When in doubt, cut me out!"

—*Entertainment Weekly,* October 25, 2002

I don't know why anybody talks to me. I wouldn't talk to me. If you see me coming, it's not a good day.

—*Detroit News,* October 25, 2002

Basically I write checks to people. They write to me, they tell me things that they're doing, and I just write them checks. I don't think it's good to have a lot of money lying around.

—In response to a question about what he does with his newfound wealth, as reported in the *Times* (London), October 25, 2002

I wouldn't [be an activist] if I didn't have some hope. The majority has never effected change anywhere in the world; it's always been a small percentage.

—*Boston Herald,* October 18, 2002

I'm really just an average citizen who decided to get involved.

—*Columbus Dispatch,* September 15, 1996

have a very wide, broad audience that goes deep into the mainstream of America, and I'm one of the few people on the left that has that, and I feel very fortunate and privileged to have it.

—*Los Angeles Times,* March 7, 2002

think everybody thinks they know me, and they can come up and let's just shoot the s——— for a while. I really respond to that, and I am really honored by it.

—*Denver Post,* September 28, 1996

No, actually, the day I passed geometry in 10th grade was the biggest day.

> —When asked by a TV station during the premiere of *Roger & Me* if this was his biggest day, as reported in the *St. Petersburg Times*, January 21, 1990

Generally speaking, I don't like documentaries. I don't like PBS. I think that stuff is pretty boring.

> —*Christian Science Monitor,* January 16, 1990

The things I want are not material. I have two pairs of jeans. If you talk to me a year from now, I'll still only have two pairs. But maybe they'll be washed more often.

—*People*, January 15, 1990

I've been with [my wife, Kathleen] for 13 years now and I am very happy and content. She was raised in a Catholic household, too. So we have the same neuroses.

—*Observer*, August 28, 1994

I may be a smart aleck, but I'm a smart aleck for the people.

—*Minneapolis Star Tribune,* September 20, 1997

I didn't make more than $17,000 a year before 1990. I lived the first 17 years of my adult life like that, and I know how to live on $17,000, and I'm not afraid of ever having to do that again. If you accept that, no one can ever have you, and you will always respond to your conscience.

—*Boston Herald,* April 11, 1999

It's a very dangerous thing to give someone like me a lot of money. Because I have so few material needs and so little desire for things, if you put that much money in my hands I am going to do a lot of damage with it. It's like handing me a Molotov cocktail.

—*Guardian* (Manchester, England),
October 4, 2003

The day after my election [to the school board], the assistant principal changed my name from "Hey, you!" to "Mr. Moore," and suddenly I realized I was in a place where maybe I could do some good.

—*Los Angeles Times,* October 3, 2003

Personally it was very difficult. I had to endure a lot of threats of violence and harassment. . . . My home was vandalized. There's a part of me that regretted saying anything because I put my family in jeopardy.

—On his life after his 2002 Oscar acceptance speech, as reported in the *Rocky Mountain News,* October 16, 2003

ON *ROGER & ME*

There's a lot of anger in *Roger & Me.* I think it's healthy to be angry. I wanted people to leave the theater being angry, not depressed. Depression just sinks you.

—*Columbus Dispatch,* September 15, 1996

[GM chairman Roger Smith] said he hasn't seen the movie yet and so I figured . . . I'll give him the very first copy of the videotape.

—*Orlando Sentinel,* June 21, 1990

It's not an NBC White Paper,
not an episode of *Nova.* To the
guardians of documentary,
I apologize that the picture
is entertaining.

—*Australian Financial Review,* May 4, 1990

Warner Brothers is not
promoting the film because they
are at the forefront of political
revolution. They're doing it because
they think it will make money.

—*Boston Globe,* April 30, 1990

Liberals and yuppies, the people who read Pauline Kael in the *New Yorker,* would prefer to see people like us as victims. They would give you images of welfare lines and unemployment lines, bag ladies, people sleeping in the street. That's what you see on the evening news. None of those images is in my movie.

—*Sunday Herald,* April 29, 1990

Any time a person comes along and tries to advance an art-form to a new phase he meets resistance from those who consider themselves the keeper of the old flame.

—*Herald,* March 23, 1990

I am partial. The film has a point of view, but I did not distort the facts or, as [critic] Harlan Jacobson says, play fast and loose with the truth in order to make my political point. There's a certain comedic license that is being taken with the film.

—*New York Times,* February 1, 1990

I guess I'd describe *Roger & Me* as a dark comedy, a cross between *Grapes of Wrath* and *Pee-wee's Big Adventure.*

—*People,* January 15, 1990

Laughter is a political tool. People get to laugh at Roger Smith and the rich in the movie. That in and of itself is a political act because there are so few avenues these days to express yourself in opposition to the status quo.

—*Newsday,* January 25, 1990

I wanted to make a film that people would watch Friday nights at the mall, to enjoy with their Goobers. I like to see movies like *Die Hard, Robocop* and *Pee-wee's Big Adventure,* not *Women on the Verge of a Nervous Breakdown.* I didn't want to make a film for the art-house crowd.

—*USA Today,* January 18, 1990

I've done no student shorts, no 8-millimeter experiments, no video. I still don't know how to set the timer on my VCR.

—*Seattle Times,* January 10, 1990

It's not going to change things tomorrow. But it's a small piece of what I hope is a much larger mosaic of people becoming active in the 1990s. That's something I would really like to see happen. And if I or this film can play a small part in that, it would be great.

—*Christian Science Monitor,*
January 16, 1990

The GM chairman recently said that he refuses to see the film because he is "not much for sick humor." Any guy who eliminates 35,000 jobs at a time when his company is making $5 billion in profits is into sick humor.

—*Macleans,* January 15, 1990

I just assume a vast number of Americans know they're getting screwed. I don't have to spend the first half hour telling them that.

—*Newsday,* December 17, 1989

I know it sounds foolish, but at the beginning, I really thought [Roger Smith] might see me. My idea was to have him come to Flint, to ride around with me in a van with the door open and the camera rolling, and I would interview him, and maybe he could explain things. I envisioned something like a *60 Minutes* interview.

—*St. Louis Post-Dispatch,* January 14, 1990

If Mr. Smith had come to Flint, I would have hoped he'd have resigned and gone to work in the soup kitchen. He needs to see the human result of the decision he made.

—*Guardian* (Manchester, England), January 12, 1990

I think that scrounging has been good for me and for the film. As much as I'd like to think that if I had been given $1 million before I started shooting that I would have made the same movie, I doubt it. There's something to be said for the struggle.

—*Chicago Tribune,* January 7, 1990

If we can pull the curtain back and see what corporate America did to Flint, then maybe viewers will wonder about their own hometown just a little.

—*San Francisco Chronicle,* January 7, 1990

I made this film for personal and political reasons. See, the homeless didn't just drop out of the sky, and we wanted to find out who was responsible. We wanted to name names.

—*New York Times,* September 28, 1989

think Roger [Smith] has said a couple of things to the press. He's said he's not going to see it because he's not going to like it. He's said he feels bad for the people of Flint because they're going to have to suffer through this movie. Hah! Suffer through this movie, and [they've got] a murder rate higher than Detroit.

—*Toronto Star,* December 16, 1989

ON *STUPID WHITE MEN*

Look, I have some empathy
for HarperCollins. There was no
playbook for how to react to Sept.
11. They were trying to find their
way forward. But how should
a publisher behave in a crisis?
Do you take the quick and easy
approach of totalitarian regimes,
or do you say, "Damnit, let's go
with the book, this is why we
have these freedoms"?

—*Philadelphia Inquirer,* January 6, 2002

People are much smarter and more liberal than you'd think. I never dreamed *Stupid White Men* would be on the best-seller list, but there it is. Don't believe most people are as right-wing as the right-wingers say. It's just not true!

—*Christian Science Monitor,*
October 4, 2002

For this book to reach No. 1, it means I'm being read by mainstream Middle America. Now, what do I do with this?

—*U.S. News & World Report,* April 1, 2002

I said [to HarperCollins]: "Let me get this straight. You want me to pay you for the right to censor myself? I'm not rewriting 50 percent of one word."

—*Rocky Mountain News,* March 7, 2002

To see this overwhelming response [to *Stupid White Men*], to see it trounce all the conservative, right-wing books on the best-seller list, tells me that there are a lot more out there of us than they think there are and that we think there are, and they don't just live in the Berkeleys and the Ann Arbors and the Madisons of this country. They're all over the place and they've had to shut up for five or six months.

—Speech before the Commonwealth Club,
March 4, 2002

ON POLITICAL PARTIES

I don't think anybody really knows what those terms [Republicans, Democrats] mean. Those two parties exist to do the bidding of the upper 10 percent, who pay them to be there, and the other 90 percent of the American public has no political party really that's a major party that's on the ballot, and I think the time is really ripe for independents.

—*Crossfire,* August 8, 2002

The Democrats and Republicans are so much alike, obediently supporting the very system that brought ruin to so many families, that the average American couldn't care less what any of them have to say. They know voting will not improve their lives, not one single bit.

—*Denver Post,* November 3, 1996

The great thing about Republicans is that even when they are caught with their pants down, they don't give a damn.

—*Pittsburgh Post-Gazette,* July 17, 1994

If the Democrats want to win, they've got to get some backbone and some spine and start acting like Democrats and not Republicans. People who like Republicans already have a party. It's called the Republican Party.

—*Lou Dobbs Tonight,* October 14, 2003

I mean, this is a party [Democratic] that can't even win when they win. They lose when they win, you can't get more pathetic than that. We have to save them from themselves.

—*Entertainment Weekly,* July 9, 2004

I see [the Democratic Party] as the problem. They create the illusion of hope. I wanted to show people [in *Roger & Me*] that this has nothing to do with Democrats or Republicans. We have a one-party system with two heads.

—*Newsday*, January 25, 1990

And Arnold [Schwarzenegger] for the first time demonstrates that the Republicans have got to become more liberal to get elected.

—*San Jose Mercury News*,
October 20, 2003

ON *TV NATION*

TV Nation was on NBC, then we were on FOX, then on Comedy Central. I could see where it was going. I didn't want to end up on the Food Channel.

—CNN.com, April 27, 1999

We sit around each week and say, "How do we get the people watching *Full House* to watch this show, because we know they'll like it. How do we get them to turn off the Olsen twins?"

—*St. Petersburg Times,* December 27, 1994

I don't believe that television is a church and I don't think people turn on television to hear sermons. If we've decided to go on television, we've decided that people should be entertained for that hour while also learning about what's going on.

—*Times* (London), July 16, 1994

On the one hand, I fear for the country. On the other, we'll need less writers for the show. The material will be written for us.

—*Boston Globe,* December 28, 1994

▌ mean, this isn't the easiest show to get into because it's its own genre; it doesn't fit into anything else, and so it's not what people are used to seeing on TV.

—*Houston Chronicle,*
December 28, 1994

▌'m not going to wait for the constitutional amendment on school prayer to pass. I'm insisting that everyone at *TV Nation* take a minute each day to pray for the country.

—*South Florida Sun-Sentinel,*
December 28, 1994

You're taking two forms that seem opposed to each other—comedy and documentary—and combining them. You're guaranteeing everything you see is true. Everything you see is as we film it. Yet we've injected our point of view and our sense of humor into the piece, so it has a sort of subversive quality to it.

—*Los Angeles Times,* July 19, 1994

They knew what they were getting into. When they asked me what I would do if they gave me an hour of TV, I thought they had the wrong person. Maybe they were looking for another Michael Moore. Maybe they were looking for Roger Moore. Or Dudley Moore. I don't know.

—*Philadelphia Daily News,* July 19, 1994

People know who I am, and they still talk to me. There's something about being on TV and in the movies that's attractive to everybody.

—*Toronto Star,* July 19, 1994

How did I get *TV Nation* on to NBC? I have no answer to that question except they are in third place and are willing to take some risks.

—*Observer,* August 28, 1994

We fall into no division at NBC: There's News, Entertainment, and Sports, and within Entertainment, there's Comedy and Drama. We're not news, but we are nonfiction, and we're entertaining, I hope. But I don't know where we belong.

—*Newsday,* July 10, 1994

WHAT OTHER PEOPLE SAY
ABOUT MICHAEL MOORE

**O**utrageously false.

—Dan Bartlett, the White House communications
director, about *Fahrenheit 9/11*'s contention
that there was a nefarious connection between
President Bush and Osama bin Laden's family,
as reported in the *New York Times,* June 20, 2004

We don't have a lot of free
time these days and when we do
have free time to see a good fiction
movie, we'll pick *Shrek* or some
other enjoyable feature like that.

—White House Communications Director
Dan Bartlett, June 25, 2004

This is not the *New York Times*; it's not a network news report. The facts have to be right, yes, but this is an individual's view of current events. And I'm a very firm believer that it is within everybody's right to examine the actions of their government.

—Dev Chatillon, former general counsel
for the *New Yorker,* as reported in the
New York Times, June 20, 2004

Michael Moore is politically irrelevant and does not have the same stature in Hollywood as Mr. Heston.

—Andrew Arulanandam, the National Rifle Association spokesman, *Daily News,* October 6, 2002

So should we sue or take out ads in the paper telling our side? Our public relations staff said not to do anything, not to make something bigger out of this than it already is.

—General Motors Chairman Roger Smith commenting on *Roger & Me,* as reported in the *Chicago Tribune,* February 10, 1990

Mr. Moore has every right to produce and show movies that express his very radical views. He's outside of the mainstream. . . . This is a film that doesn't require us to actually view it to know it's filled with factual inaccuracies.

—White House Communications Director
Dan Bartlett, June 25, 2004

Our legal department is thrilled to be working with Michael.

—Ed Carroll, executive vice president and
general manager of Bravo and the
Independent Film Channel, as reported in
the *Dallas Morning News,* January 21, 1999